after the fire

ALSO BY J. A. JANCE

after the fire
J. A. JANCE

WILLIAM MORROW

An Imprint of HarperCollinsPublishers

First published in 2004 by the University of Arizona Libraries. Poems originally published in 1984 by Lance Publications.

HarperCollins books may be purchased for educational, business, or sales promotional use. For information please write: Special Markets Department, HarperCollins Publishers, 10 East 53rd Street, New York, NY 10022.

FIRST WILLIAM MORROW EDITION PUBLISHED 2013.

Designed by Lisa Stokes

Library of Congress Cataloging-in-Publication Data has been applied for.

ISBN 978-0-06-229397-8

13 14 15 16 17   OV/BVG   10 9 8 7 6 5 4 3 2 1

DEDICATION, FIRST EDITION: **FOR J.J.T.J.**

If it weren't for the rocks in its bed, the stream would have no song.

DEDICATION, SECOND EDITION: **FOR W.A.S.**

Thanks for making the second half of my life happy. It turns out there are still songs, even when there are no rocks.

DEDICATION, THIRD EDITION: **FOR ALICE.**

Thanks for bringing it home.

Contents

Preface

This book of poetry is also a book about addiction and the insidious way in which it destroys relationships. On the surface, one might think it is only about my first husband's eventually fatal relationship with alcohol. But it is also, just as clearly, the story of my own addiction—the one that linked me to my husband and to my own unwavering determination to save him from himself, whether or not he wanted to be saved. It is a story of hurt and loss and betrayal. It is also a story of hope.

It was 1968 when I first began writing these poems. I was a twenty-four-year-old newlywed who had written a children's book that garnered a kind letter from an editor at a New York publishing house. The editor told me that if I was willing to make changes in the manuscript, she would consider publishing it. Thrilled, I showed the letter to my husband, expecting him to be as happy about it as I was. Instead, the letter provoked a firefight. My husband, who had been allowed into a university-level creative writing class that had been closed to me, took a dim view of the possibility that some of my work might be published.

"There's only going to be one writer in our family," he told me. "And I am it."

The way he said the words made it clear that if I wanted to preserve our marriage, I would put my writing ambitions away and leave them there. Which is what I did—for the next fourteen years.

In a way neither of us understood, my husband's "one writer" statement was correct. There would be only one published writer in our family, but he wasn't it. Although he wrote constantly, scribbling columns across page after page of graph paper, nothing that came from his hand ever made it into actual print. He was content to imitate Faulkner and Hemingway primarily by drinking too much and writing too little, but at the time he laid down the law, I was still utterly dazzled by his self-proclaimed potential.

The one thing that separates writers from other people is that they write. From 1968 to 1973, my husband and I were teachers in Sells, Arizona, on the Tohono O'odham reservation west of Tucson. He taught high school English and Spanish while I was a K–12 librarian. We lived in a little rented house on King's Anvil Ranch, thirty miles east of Sells near the community of Three Points. The closest neighbor and/or telephone was literally miles away.

On those long, solitary evenings, after my husband fell asleep— No, wait. What's surprising to me is that even all these years later, my first instinct is still to minimize how bad things were back then, but that's how denial works. What I should have said is: On those long, solitary evenings, after my husband passed out in front of the blaring television set, there was no one for me to talk to and very little to keep me occupied. Married but essentially alone, I turned to writing poetry. Initially I thought what I was doing was art, plain and simple. Poetry offered a way of looking at ordinary objects or events and turning them into something beautiful. That's how the poems in this book started—as "art."

The poetry was written over the course of several years. The various verses were jotted down on stray pieces of lined yellow paper and tossed into the strongbox that also held our birth certificates and marriage certificate. Eventually it would hold our children's birth certificates as well. At that point in my life I was incapable of seeing that I was using poetry as a prism through which to examine what was going on in my own life. The artifice of "art" allowed me to maintain emotional distance. I could look at what was happening without ever having to come to terms with what was going on in my marriage. It spared me the harsh reality and hard work of actually doing something to change our disaster-bound direction. Looking at my poetry with the benefit of hindsight, I see how, as early as 1968, a part of me understood that my marriage was doomed, even though I was a good twelve years from admitting it or taking appropriate and necessary action.

Eighteen months after I finally got a divorce, within a few minutes of midnight on New Year's Eve 1982, my first husband died of chronic alcoholism at age forty-two. His death sent me back to the strongbox, looking for those important pieces of paper death requires: birth certificates for him and for our two children, along with our marriage certificate and my divorce decree. There, lurking among those official documents, I found the collection of scribbled poems. Reading through them in 1983 was like seeing my life in instant replay. I could recall where I was when I wrote each individual poem and what events had provoked it. Other people reading the poems urged me to try to publish them, and I did. *After the Fire* came out in 1984 under the auspices of a small Seattle-area publisher.

In June 1985, I did one of my first poetry readings at a retreat sponsored by Widowed Information Consultation Services of King County (WICS). It was there that I met a man whose first wife had succumbed to breast cancer after seven years of debilitating illness. She died within a few minutes of midnight on New Year's Eve 1984. Her grieving husband and I struck up a conversation based on the shared coincidence of having a spouse die on New Year's Eve. Our similar experiences with a dying spouse led quickly to an extraordinary closeness. Six months later, to the dismay of our five adolescent children, we told them, "You're not the Brady Bunch, but you'll do," and we got married. That was twenty-eight years, several weddings, six grandchildren, and many dogs ago. But it's why I consider *After the Fire* to be my most important book—the one that changed the course of my life for the better.

In the years since then, while writing and publicizing my mysteries, I've squeezed in a few poetry readings along the way. At readings I've tried to give my audience the background stories and to tell them where I was and what was going on in my life when I wrote the various poems.

People often tell me that the poetry has touched them and that my story has spoken to them and resonated in a very personal way. They confide that many of the same things happened to them. Several have even written to say that *After the Fire* inspired them to make much-needed changes in their own lives.

Several months ago, the latest version of the book went out of print and all rights to it reverted to me. Since that time any number of people have asked when the poetry would once again be available; a version with the background stories brought current seemed to be in order.

The poems here are, with one exception, arranged in chronological order—the way I wrote them and the way I lived them as well. I have written some poetry since 1984, but not much. For one thing, I've been too busy and far too happy. For me, writing poetry and being happy don't seem to mix.

If there's a message in all this, I want it to be one of encouragement to those who are themselves caught up in impossible relationships. I hope the book speaks to some of those folks who have lost all hope and who believe that, for them, nothing will ever be better. Ozymandias may have said, "Look on my works, ye mighty, and despair." I say, "Look on mine and know things can be better."

after the fire

A Question of Gender

In the late 1960s and early 1970s, I was caught up in the women's movement. I read Simone de Beauvoir, Betty Friedan, and Gloria Steinem. I also burned a bra, but that's another story. At the time, it was easier for me to be mad at all men in general than it was for me to take a close look at the particular man to whom I was married.

While I was working on the Tohono O'odham reservation, a friend and I drove more than two hundred miles after school one afternoon to hear Gloria Steinem speak. She was funny, intelligent, and witty. Throughout the talk, my friend, a Native American and the mother of five, a woman who had never lived off the reservation, laughed at all the jokes and nodded in agreement.

When we left the hall after the speech, my friend turned to me and said, "I always thought it was because I was an Indian."

As we used to say back in those days, "Click!"

A QUESTION OF GENDER

To speak, to hear, to know
For the first time that the problem
Is not to be Black or White or Indian
But to be woman, female,
And all the other ugly epithets—
Broad, bitch, whore—
That go with being born
Without a penis.

There is strength and hope
In knowing that the common denominator
Is, in fact, a caprice of nature,
A simple matter of plumbing.
And once the knowledge that the problem
Is not singular but is the birthright
Of half the world's population—
Once that knowledge sinks in—
What follows will make
The shot heard round the world
Seem a mere firecracker.

Morning

My husband was a beginning high school English teacher and I a school librarian. There wasn't much money to start with, but my husband drank prodigiously, which made our financial situation even more precarious. For me, staying home and raising kids was never the same kind of option that it had been for my mother, who, it turned out, had managed to stay home and raise seven kids on even less money, but with a husband—my father—who wasn't a drinker and who brought his paychecks home instead of cashing them at bars. Years later, on a Sunday afternoon, my five-year-old son would ask, "But, Dad, why don't you go to a bank to cash a check?" It was a good question—one I should have been asking my husband a long time earlier.

As a relative newlywed, I tried to imagine what it would be like to be able to stay home and look after children. Since such an existence didn't seem to be in the cards for me, I managed to convince myself that I wouldn't be any good at it. Besides, I was a college graduate. Wouldn't my education be wasted if I did nothing but stay home? It was what my mother did, but she had no more than a seventh-grade education. Certainly her headstrong daughter could do better than that!

For years I prided myself on the fact that, since my daughter was born at the beginning of Christmas vacation, I missed only three days of school due to childbirth. Forty-plus years later, I no longer see that in such a positive light.

Are there important mother-daughter issues behind much of my early poetry? Absolutely. Those same issues are at work in some of my novels as well, but in this particular poem, the cigarette was what made all the difference. The woman in the poem and I both drink coffee, but because she smoked and I didn't, I was able to distance myself from her. I was not the frustrated housewife and mother pictured in this poem. She and I weren't one. Her unhappiness and mine didn't mesh and mingle.

Now I know otherwise.

MORNING

This is the time when, according to the media,
She is supposed to settle back and relax
Over a cigarette and a second cup of coffee,
Receiving a much-deserved rest after bundling
Children and husband off to school and office.
What Madison Avenue cannot know
Is how bleak and empty
The day stretches out through
The steam of that second cup of coffee,
Filled with mindless tasks,
Endlessly repeated.
Is this all?

Bitter Fruit

In 1968 I was still smarting over my husband's decree that I not rewrite the manuscript for my children's book and submit it for publication. Of course, had I really been the fire-breathing feminist I thought myself to be, I would have told him to take a hike. Instead, I bowed to his wishes and put the manuscript away. (That story was eventually rewritten, and published in 1985 under the title "It's Not Your Fault" as part of a children's personal safety series.)

I began writing poems on those long, solitary nights and stowing them away before I went to bed. Instinctively understanding how explosive my illicit writing was, I never showed any of my poems to my husband. Looking back, I believe that's about the time my anger began to build, too. In this poem in particular, I can almost smell the smoke from that slow burn of resentment that would smolder for the next dozen years before finally bursting into flame.

They say that living well is the best revenge. At the time of this writing, in the spring of 2013, my forty-fifth murder mystery has debuted at number 12 on the *New York Times* Best Sellers List. In 2000, the University of Arizona, where I was once denied admittance to creative writing classes on the basis of my being a "girl," granted me an honorary doctorate of humane letters. These days, that once bitter fruit has a much sweeter taste, and there is more than enough irony to go around.

But there is someone else's story hidden in the background of this poem—that of a friend, a Native American woman with several small children and a ne'er-do-well husband (I could see that her husband was bad news!), who wanted to have her tubes tied but couldn't have the procedure performed without her husband's written permission, which he, of course, refused to grant.

BITTER FRUIT

It is a slow dawning,
This realization of existence
On a leash.
        Of making excuses
For thoughts and actions
That were never really executed.

It is a slow awakening,
This knowledge that your life
Is a compromise
        Of other people's
Intentions of what shall be done
With your flesh and bones.

Yes, and mind too, although
Nobody ever intimated that you
Might be possessed
        Of one of those
For intellect has always been
A masculine demesne.

But with the dawning, the realization,
That you, a newborn Eve, have tried
The bitter fruit
            Of knowledge,
Can you then, content, go back
To live the plastic lie you were before?

No.

Shifting Gears

I was a girl who grew up in the 1950s. The vast majority of women from that era came complete with a panoply of mixed messages. This was a time when girls who wanted to become doctors became nurses; girls who wanted to become engineers became high school geometry teachers; girls who wanted to become ministers became ministers' wives; and girls who wanted to become writers married men who were allowed into creative writing programs that were closed to women. We saw the inequities, but for the most part we went along with the program, kept our mouths shut, and did what was expected—which is how, after being locked out of the creative writing program at the University of Arizona, I ended up being first a high school English teacher and later a school librarian.

In the 1960s I began reading those dangerous consciousness-raising books, and eventually things did change. So, yes, I did burn a bra—a nursing bra. When you burn a bra, the whole idea is to have it blaze up in a satisfying conflagration. Due to my own ambivalence, however, I didn't toss my bra onto the barbecue grill until *after* I had finished cooking dinner. By the time I got around to making my political statement, the coals had cooled down. Instead of flaming up and incinerating, my bra simply charred around the edges of the foam rubber, which pretty much detracted from the desired effect.

At the time I was chagrined that the bra didn't burn. In retrospect, I see that charred hulk as a reflection of the terrible dichotomy in my life—a longing to be set free of the old ways while still standing mired knee-deep in the muck.

The old adage is still true: You can't have your cake and eat it, too. In this case, more fittingly, it would have to be: You can't cook dinner and burn your bra, too.

SHIFTING GEARS

The danger lies not as the broadcasters
    would have you believe,
In the burning of a few extraneous and uncomfortable
    undergarments.

It lies in the fact that women can lay down
    their weapons,
The perfumes and fineries with which they have
    armed themselves,

And come together in friendship to speak, console,
    and even love
Each other as they have never done before.
    Now they can

Simply refuse to scratch each other's eyes out so
    that some man
Can have the pleasure of possessing the scarred body
    of the winner.

Strangers

We're back to the mother-daughter issue again. My mother dropped out of school in seventh grade because her vision was bad. She needed glasses to see the blackboard, and there was no money in her family for glasses. She went to Minneapolis to work as a maid for a cartoonist and his invalid wife. Later she married my father and raised seven children—washing clothes, ironing, and cooking three meals a day at a time when there were no automatic clothes washers or dryers and no dishwashers or microwaves, either.

Growing up, I was a bookworm. My mother read magazines—when she had time, that is. With all the unyielding arrogance of the young, I was contemptuous of her for not sharing my love of books. By the time I reached high school, my two older sisters had both married, one during high school and one immediately after graduation. Hoping for a different result, my mother encouraged me to take a heavy class load—six solid credits, as they were called back then, and one non-solid, music. My mother's encouragement came in the form of a bribe. She said that if I took extra classes she would exempt me from the household chores she had required of my older sisters.

I was six feet tall and wore thick glasses, which set me well out-side the in-crowd of my high school's "cool" social circle. I was also bookish and more than a little lazy. I didn't think twice before accept-ing my mother's offer, one which set me on an academic track in high school and led, eventually, to a scholarship and to my admission to college.

I wouldn't be where I am today without having had the advantage of what my mother did for me back then. When I wrote this poem, in my midtwenties, I was not yet a mother and had no real appreciation for what my mother had done for all her children through the years.

Now I'm a mother and a grandmother, too. It's safe to say I'm over it. Not over the need to demand equal rights and responsibilities for everyone, but over being blind to women's very real contributions to society whether in or out of the workplace.

By the way, if you have read my Joanna Brady books, your suspi-cions are hereby confirmed. Yes, you have met my mother—a version of her anyway—in Joanna Brady's mother, Eleanor Lathrop Winfield.

STRANGERS

My hopes and fears are alien to her.
When we speak, it is as though our words
Come from two different languages
With no hope of finding an interpreter
To reconcile them.

She has lived her life by the old rules—
Spent her time cooking, cleaning, bearing children.
My abandonment of the kitchen
She regards as the ultimate treachery,
A final defection.

I see her as "just a housewife";
See her years as mother a waste
Of human potential, of intellect, of being.
Until we both can look at one another
With minds washed clean of prejudice,
Until we can see the difference and the value
Of both separate lives, it will be
Impossible for my mother and me
To be sisters.

Choices

I was a smart girl at a time when being smart and female wasn't a particularly good idea. I figured out fairly early in the game that I was smarter than my first husband, who also happens to have been the first man I ever dated. Not wanting to rock the boat, I tried not to make an issue of it. For his part, my husband did what he could to keep me in my place.

In his defense, I have to say that my husband was living according to the script he had learned at his own mother's knee. She told me once, when I was single-handedly supporting the family by working as a district manager in the life insurance business—that "it's all right if a woman works to help her husband support the family, but it certainly isn't all right if she makes more money than he does."

Given that kind of background, it's hardly surprising that her son was less than enthusiastic about my getting my master's of education degree in 1970. One way of showing his displeasure was to take the position that graduation ceremonies were stupid and were to be avoided at all costs. Deflated by his lack of enthusiasm, I skipped commencement and received my diploma by mail. When I started taking classes toward my CLU (chartered life underwriter) designation in the insurance business, my husband always managed to provoke some kind of crisis right around the time I had to be either attending classes or taking an exam. Several of his nine stints in rehab happened either before or immediately after scheduled exams.

Is the next poem about us? It wasn't consciously at the time I wrote it, because I was still doing "art." In retrospect, I can say absolutely that we were the subject.

Incidentally, years later, when the University of Arizona awarded my honorary doctorate, I was there to pick it up. The rest of my family was there as well, including my then eighty-five-year-old mother.

CHOICES

She wore ambition like a double-breasted suit,
Well-tailored but a little long.
She sought her chosen goal with firm resolve,
Detouring at times, but never straying far.

He was a dashing, happy youth
Whose cheery laughter and romantic ways
Charmed her to believe her solitary path
Could easily be trod by two.

But he, without her clear-eyed vision and determined air,
Grew weary when her beacon failed to dim.
He counted treachery among her notes and books
And hated every study she pursued.

She walks alone now, having paid
A price the world does not require from any man
Who sets ambition over hearth and home.
Thank God she hasn't given up the fight.

Best Friends

For eighteen years I deluded myself into thinking I was woman enough to keep my man.

I didn't find out how wrong that assumption had been until much later. Five years after my divorce, I discovered that, despite the fact I had been faithful during my marriage and celibate after it ended, I was suffering from a sexually transmitted disease.

Given all that, one would think that the next poem is about me. Again, it wasn't—at least not consciously so.

To my way of thinking, I was writing "Best Friends" about a friend from college—a woman whose marriage to one of our classmates had recently collapsed into divorce due to the fact that her husband—who could well have been a clone of my own spouse—was fooling around with other women, including one of his wife's best friends. With the benefit of hindsight, it's possible to see that this poem was about both of us. Unfortunately, it reflects the experience of far too many other women as well.

BEST FRIENDS

Did you say he was the first?
So what? Is that why you're still hanging on,
Pretending that he's everything you want?

You don't have to pay with your whole life.
That debt was canceled long ago,
Interest, principal, and all.

Your virgin loyalty has led you down
A primrose path and kept you bound
Beyond the call of reason.

Stay if you want to,
But not because he took you first.
For him you weren't the last.
Don't ask me how I know.

Misgivings

My younger sister came to visit, bringing the unwelcome news that she was dropping out of college to marry her boyfriend. With the unerring fallibility of our mother's daughters, my sister's first choice was a troubled piece of humanity who wasn't worth the powder it would have taken to blow him up. Looking at him, I could clearly see that she was casting her pearls before swine. Of course it was easy for me to see everything wrong with her future husband and nothing at all wrong with mine. My husband was perfectly fine, but I didn't want my sister to mess up her own life by making some idiotic mistake.

I believe there's a passage in the Bible that speaks to this—something about seeing the mote in someone else's eye while being blind to the boulder in one's own. This was definitely the case when I wrote this poem. It gives me no pleasure forty years later to realize how right I was.

My sister's first husband is long gone, of course, but then so is mine.

MISGIVINGS

It frightens me to see her,
Trembling on the brink of life
And love.
             I want to reach out,
To help, to offer her a hand
And guide her from the precipice.

Yet I'm frightened, too, of being rebuffed,
Afraid that she'll disdain the offerings
My slim experience can bestow.
Afraid that she will damn me
For my meddling and ignore
The warnings, the cautions that
My heart cries out to give.

But still I know that she
Must make her own way blindly,
Although we who have gone before
Long to give her the newfound vision
We have of this world.

She must, at last, make her own way.
And so, old fool, leave off
Your dire mutterings of heartache and disaster
And wish her luck and happiness
And love.

Portrait

For Christmas the year after we married, my first husband gave me a Kenmore sewing machine—not the top-of-the-line zigzag model, but the loss-leader, straight-stitch, $39.95 version. I never succeeded in making it work properly, which was no doubt due to operator ineptitude. At last I closed the lid, shutting the machine inside, and relegated the wooden cabinet to the role of side table. Upon this ungainly piece of furniture sat a gold-framed photograph—an eight-by-ten portrait of me wearing my wedding dress.

The wedding had been cobbled together in a hurry. On New Year's Day 1967, my fiancé made me an offer I couldn't refuse: "If you can have the wedding organized in time, we can be married over semester break." I had been waiting more than five years to hear those words, and after he said them, you couldn't see me for the dust. On January 29, less than a month later, we tied the knot. I was a first-year teacher and my husband was a student. That made us poor. The wedding was a bargain-basement affair. The wedding dress cost $125. Flowers for everyone came to a total of $30. All photographs, including the one on the dead sewing machine, were taken by a team of camera-wielding friends.

For me this poem is interesting in terms of both what it says and what it leaves out. The picture was taken in a church social hall. The amateur photographer posed me in front of a basement wall. The problem is, the wall contained a padlocked door that led to a storage room. The photograph plainly captures the brass lock. Not surprisingly, it is missing from this wistful study of the image. Instead, using my poetic license as a blinder, I managed to ignore the bad omen that locked padlock really represented.

PORTRAIT

The lace is there, white and flowing to a train
From the slender waist.
The breasts are young and firm,
Expectant under a well-fitting bodice.
Studying the picture closely, one expects
To see those breasts rise and fall in lightly taken breaths.

The hands, demure, are almost invisible
Beneath a cascade of white flowers,
For no sacrifice would be complete
Without flowers to lend their perfume
To the memorable occasion.

A slender neck, bedecked with antique pearls,
A slight smile, a veil of cloudy lace.
How long before that smile lies buried
Beneath a hundred petty tyrannies?

Entrapment

It is disturbing to realize that "Portrait" and the next two poems, "Entrapment" and "Idle Conversation," all predate my divorce by ten years and two children. The children, you see, were part of my overall game plan. In fact, they were my two highest face cards.

I had set out on a single-minded crusade to save the man I loved from himself. For years he had assured me that he would stop drinking once we had children. To my credit, I had some reason to believe him. His father had been drunk when he went away to World War II and had come back sober. To my knowledge, my father-in-law never had another drink, and he never went to meetings, either. My father-in-law told me several times not to worry, that when his son was ready to straighten up he would. It turned out my husband wasn't made of quite the same stuff as his father.

Totally unaware that my husband was incapable of keeping his promise, I spent the first five years of our marriage hoping beyond hope that we would get pregnant. Each month when that didn't happen, I was plunged into a pit of despair.

When I wrote "Entrapment," I had never lived anywhere but Arizona and had never visited the fish ladder at the Chittenden Locks in Seattle. Years later, when I did go there, I was shocked by the battered condition of the fish I saw. The salmon simile was far more appropriate for what was happening in my life than I could possibly have imagined.

And yes, in those days, that's exactly what a marriage license cost in Tucson, Arizona—two bucks.

ENTRAPMENT

If there were some definite way of knowing,
The report of a rifle, a shotgun blast,
That would tell her precisely when
The trap was sprung, it might be
Somewhat easier to deal with the shambles
Her life has, before her very eyes, become.

There was no clang of iron gates
When he slipped the yellow band
Upon a willing finger. If only
They had posted danger signs in that
Dingy office where, for only two dollars,
She had signed away her life.

But no, she had been eager enough,
And even had the danger signal warned her,
She would not have listened, seen, or noticed,
But plunged on, like a salmon rushing upstream,
Bent on procreation and destruction.

Idle Conversation

For five years we lived on a hill thirty miles from town and seven miles from the nearest neighbor. After dinner, my husband would sit in his recliner and fall asleep, leaving me with an empty evening in which I could write poetry, read a book, or watch TV.

As far as television was concerned, I watched whatever I wanted because I could change the channel whenever I liked. During those times when my husband went through treatment, his homecomings were always punctuated by ferocious fights when he was awake and wanted to select the programs. Over time I had grown accustomed to keeping my own company in the evenings, to doing things my way without having to take his likes or dislikes into consideration. I know it was stressful for him to try to stop drinking. It was equally stressful for me to try to live with him when he was sober.

Again, dealing with hindsight, I can see that would have been an excellent time for me to have given Al-Anon a try, but I was in denial. Going to Al-Anon would have meant admitting there was a problem. It would also have meant that my parents had been right all along. The first time I brought my new boyfriend home to visit, my parents

warned me he was an alcoholic. I arrogantly replied that, as teetotal-
ers, they didn't know what they were talking about. True, living with
a drunk wasn't easy, but it was a hell of a lot easier than admitting I
had been wrong.

So I hung in there. The fiction in this poem, like the missing pad-
lock in "Portrait," is the newspaper. My husband was never sober long
enough to read newspapers in the evenings.

I'm smiling as I write this because I'm astonished by two
things—my stubbornness and my stupidity. I can't figure out which
came first or played the most important part. It's one of those chicken-
and-egg questions that will never have a definitive answer.

IDLE CONVERSATION

"Do you love me?" he asks.
"Yes." The answer is simple.
She has given the required response
A thousand times before, and
It is the truth, although perhaps
The truth is no longer so simple.

"Yes," she answers. "But . . ."
The last is an afterthought she hadn't planned
To loose upon the air, upon his heart or on hers.
She quails as the word falls between them. "But."
She hopes he will not notice,
Has forgotten his absentminded question
And will miss the terrifying thoughts
Behind her half-uttered answer.

His head comes up slowly.
The word has registered and she knows
She will be trapped into saying
What she herself does not yet fully understand.
"But I love myself better," she adds after a pause.

He watches her for a time, puzzled,
Pulling his eyes from the newspaper for once
To study her with knitted brows.

Perhaps for a moment he senses
The lightly veiled threat behind her words.
But then, seeing his doll alive, unchanged,
Still in her accustomed chair,
He is, at least for now, reassured.
She is making a joke,
Showing him she has kept some semblance
Of the wit she had when he married her.
He smiles at her little jest
And then returns to the real world
Of headlines and disasters.

She sits awhile longer wondering:
Is it true? Can I give more to myself
And less to him whose life is welded to mine
By a coat of living chain mail?
The answers are too staggering to consider.
She sighs and rises. "I'm going to bed,"
She says, knowing, with sinking heart,
That he will follow.

Homestead Revisited

There's a ten-year pause between "Idle Conversation" and "Homestead Revisited." The pause included a change in career—from being a school librarian to selling life insurance—and five physical moves—from Arizona to Washington, from Washington back to Bisbee, from Bisbee to Tucson, from Tucson to Phoenix, and finally from Phoenix to Seattle. That time frame also included the births of my two children. All this was done in the company of a man who was gradually sinking deeper and deeper into the depths of alcoholism.

Being both a working mother and the wife of an increasingly childlike husband didn't leave much room for writing poetry. I took it up again once I was in Phoenix and looking down the barrel of having to get a divorce. Now there was no longer any pretense of the writing being artistic—it was all too personal and painful.

While living in Phoenix, I made a solitary trek back to Three Points one day to see the house where my husband and I had lived during the five years we taught on the reservation—the rough cottage we had rented for forty dollars a month when we were first married.

For me, going back in 1982 to what we had called "The Hill" was not a happy homecoming.

HOMESTEAD REVISITED

A windswept house on barren lava flow
Surveys the desert floor for miles around.
To this unlikely spot whose beauty none but we
Could well discern, we brought our new-made vows
And love.

We were each other's all in all.
It was enough, at least at first.
Then small erosions came
To sweep us from our perch.
The house still stands. Only we
Are gone.

The Rival

Because I was still operating under the mistaken impression that I was "woman enough to keep my man," I assumed that my husband's love of booze was the only problem in our marriage. I erroneously believed that having another woman competing for my husband's affections would somehow be less hurtful than fighting a losing battle with the bottle of vodka that sat in plain sight on the kitchen counter.

I see now that "The Rival" paints a simplistic picture of something that was, in fact, far more complicated.

THE RIVAL

My rival is a fiery, golden dame
Whose wanton touch caresses care away
And makes a stranger of my lover's heart and soul.

I've battled her head-on with blazing words,
But always he returns to her embrace.
Victorious, she smiles and grants him sweet oblivion
While I, defeated and bereft,
Seek solace in a solitary bed.

Missed Connections

Anyone who has had the misfortune of spending time living with an addict knows the pain of readily broken promises and the misery of glib, meaningless apologies. "When I get home, we'll go to the Dairy Queen." Or to the fair. Or to the mall. Or we'll fly a kite. Or read a book. No promise is too small to be broken, or too large; too trivial, or too important. Broken promises are the building blocks of the cancer that eats away at marriages and severs the fragile relationships between parents and children. And like the final straw that breaks the camel's back, there is always that one last broken promise—the one that is, in fact, the very last one.

MISSED CONNECTIONS

I meant to . . .
        I'm sorry.
I forgot . . .
        I'm sorry.
I overlooked . . .
        I'm sorry.
I didn't notice . . .
        I'm sorry.
It's too late.
It's over.
        I'm sorry.

Hidden Agenda

I'm Scandinavian. I don't usually shout or throw things when I am angry. Instead, I do a slow, silent burn. And, like a placidly serene Mount Saint Helens, sitting on that core of molten lava, I'm building up to a pyroclastic blast. When I finally cut loose, watch out.

In this case, the newspaper isn't fiction at all—it's clear reporting. By gobbling up what was going on in other people's lives, I hid from what was going on in my own. Denial again. I was an expert in denial. I had to be. Otherwise, I would've had to do something about it, and I wasn't ready.

HIDDEN AGENDA

For years I have concealed
My anger behind the trembling barrier
Of a newspaper, always wondering,
With some dismay, why the white heat
From my heart failed to sear the newsprint
Into leaping flames.

Breakage

Imagine a flawless day in Phoenix in early April. It was Sunday afternoon. I had come home from church with the kids only to find the doorknobs of my house coated with olive oil. My husband explained that one of my relatives had told him a passage in the book of Revelation suggests that putting olive oil on doors will drive evil spirits away.

The evil spirit in question was the young female boarder I had taken in. A recent divorcée, she needed a place to stay, and we needed the money. She was also my ace in the hole. I was selling life insurance. It's a profession that often requires nighttime appointments. As a district manager, supervising other agents, I needed a good deal of flexibility to come and go. I didn't dare leave the kids at home alone with their father, but it was virtually impossible to hire babysitters to care for children in a house that was also home to a drunken adult male. Naturally my husband hated the boarder. She was my ticket out.

So I came home, struggled to open the greasy doorknob, and then went looking for an explanation. Once my husband told me what was up, I lost it. Completely. He disappeared into the bedroom and collapsed in a drunken stupor. I was outraged—a wild woman! *Diary of a Mad Housewife* had nothing on me. I wound up out in the backyard, heaving his half-filled booze bottles against the side of the house. Then, realizing how dangerous it was for him to be there when I was that crazy, I went into the house and called a doctor.

Admittedly, I'm the one who could have used locking up at that point. My husband was harmlessly passed out; I was the one on a rampage, but if I went to the hospital, who would care for the children? Not my husband—he was too drunk. And not the boarder, either. The olive oil ruse had worked. Scared to death, she was packing to leave. So I did the only sensible thing. After convincing a doctor to admit my husband to a mental health facility, I woke him and persuaded him to take a shower that was four days overdue. Then, like someone taking an old dog to the vet to be put down, I coaxed him into going for a ride and delivered him to the hospital.

BREAKAGE

The bottle shattered as it hit the wall.
I stood with arm upraised and knew
That I had smashed it.
It could as easily have been his head.

The anger raged around me like a roaring flood,
Filling my heart with murderous intent.
I wanted victims and it wasn't hard
To flush them from their hidden lairs.

I broke the bottles one by one with cool deliberation.
By the very act of breaking them
I certified their victory.

I took him to the doctor then,
Not because he needed it.
I did.

Dirge

One further note about denial. I had always heard that alcoholics hide their drinks. Because my husband kept his bottle of vodka right there on the kitchen counter, I deluded myself into believing the situation was less serious than it really was. (It turned out there were a lot of other bottles hidden around the house, and I had only just started discovering them.)

I kept minimizing how critical things were even after he went into DTs in late 1972, days after our daughter was born. At the time, we spent five days without sleeping because he was convinced that there were bugs crawling all over him and there were spies with complicated, high-tech listening devices hearing everything we said via a secret listening post down by the *charco,* a watering hole, a mile away. Even though he spent one whole afternoon playing chess with and talking to an opponent I couldn't hear or see, I stuck it out because I thought he was really quitting. When he started drinking again, three weeks later, my hopes were crushed. The problem is, all of that happened seven years before that April afternoon when I broke the bottles.

What finally pushed me over the edge? A number of things. Yes, there was the olive oil, but there was also the time my husband showed up at my six-year-old son's T-ball game so drunk at five o'clock in the afternoon that when the game was over he had to crawl from the bleachers to the car on his hands and knees. I was there with my children, with my children's friends, and with my children's friends' parents. And there was my husband, crawling like a baby on all fours.

In cartoons, when a character has a sudden epiphany, a lightbulb magically appears over his head. That afternoon the lightbulb came on for me. From then on nothing was ever the same. The roller coaster had inched its way to the top of the grade and then, for even longer, had clung there, poised on the pinnacle. Now it was ready to plunge to the bottom.

In the early eighties, getting a divorce was the last thing I wanted to do, but I knew it was what I had to do in order to save myself and to save my children.

DIRGE

I live a life of unrequited loss,
Of loss undignified and unfulfilled.
I bear the burden of a private pain
And crave the comfort of a public grief.

But yet I have no heart to walk away.
My pride could not endure such crass defeat.
I cling instead to pain—I know it well—
And to a fading hope that I can win.

Watershed

Things were bad. My husband had moved from the bedroom into the part of the house that had been occupied by my now long-gone boarder. We were still married, but I could no longer stand to be in the same room with him or to eat at the same table. I was walking around in a world of hurt, trying to make sense of all the awful things that had happened over the course of several incomprehensible weeks.

As I was pouring out my troubles to a friend one day, she asked me if I knew what was going to happen next. I told her I had no idea.

"Your husband has propositioned a friend, and she turned him down. He's propositioned you, and you've given him the same answer. What do you think the chances are that he might molest your daughter?"

It was a question that shocked me to my very core. Having been molested myself at age seven, I was terrified that the same thing might happen to my daughter. I have no proof that it ever did happen, but when my friend asked the question, that outcome wasn't at all outside the realm of possibility. I could not, in all honesty, say, "Absolutely not! Such a thing could never happen!" Because, somehow, I was afraid it could.

I left the restaurant then and went home, where I picked the fight that would propel my husband out of the house. It wasn't hard. All I had to do was take a little bit of the anger off the top. Mount Saint Helens was waiting underneath, ready to do the rest.

WATERSHED

The quarrel, once enjoined, immediately escalated
To atomic proportions, leaving us
No alternative but to retreat
To opposite ends of the house.

There, in separate rooms, we contemplate
Our wounds and know the breach is made,
The die is cast, and the Rubicon,
Although not altogether crossed,
Is lapping eagerly around our necks.

Moving Out

Most of my friends and relations hadn't been at that fateful T-ball game to see my husband on his hands and knees. So when I started divorce proceedings, several of these well-meaning folks showed up on my doorstep, Bibles in hand, to tell me that the unbelieving spouse could surely be saved by the believing one if I'd just shape up and pray harder. The problem was, by then I was beyond praying.

I still loved my husband, but I knew that I couldn't save him and save myself, too. I wrote "Moving Out" in the afternoon of moving day, while he was loading his boxes into his 1956 GMC pickup truck and getting ready to drive away.

MOVING OUT

I will not be the price of your redemption.
I will not pay my life to ransom yours.
Survival is the thing that I must cling to.
It's you or me now. I have made the choice.

There are those who say abandonment is sinful,
Who preach at me to end my errant ways.
Their threats of condemnation hold no terror.
Hell can't be worse than living through this day.

Reproach hangs heavy as you pack your boxes,
Separating ours to yours and mine.
Don't let me stop him, God, don't let me stop him.
Don't let me weaken. If I do, I'll die.

The Collector

I cannot tell you the exact date my husband moved out. More than thirty years later, I know it must've been a Tuesday night, because I wrote the next poem, "The Collector," after coming home from grocery shopping on Wednesday morning. Pushing a cart, I had raced through the store with tears streaming down both cheeks, not buying all the things I used to buy for him. I'm sure people who saw me in that state must have suspected me of being an escaped mental patient. And how, you might ask, do I know for certain that it was Wednesday morning when I went grocery shopping? Easy. Wednesday was double-stamp day.

I believe this poem is a benchmark. It shows how low I was in early March 1980. Please remember that, other than that one unpublished children's book and my furtive bits of scribbled poetry, I had yet to do any serious writing. I am preparing this new edition of *After the Fire* in the spring of 2013. It's thirty-three years since I went shopping on that fateful Wednesday morning. My marriage had failed, and I thought my life was over. I wasn't dead, but I fervently wished I was. Now that my forty-sixth novel is due to be published this fall, good friends like to mimic that old Virginia Slims commercial when they tell me, "You've come a long way, baby."

One last side note. My mother saved Gold Bond Stamps, which is probably why I gravitated to S&H Green Stamps. Unfortunately, trading stamps really did go out of style, but some people never change. Now, instead of saving Green Stamps, I am into frequent-flier miles. So are my daughters.

DNA is like that.

THE COLLECTOR

I like the green ones best.
I count them up as any miser would
And watch them grow with satisfaction,
For they are the tangible symbol
Of what is processed here—
Toilet paper, lettuce, pork and beans.
The taxes must be paid in cash.
God knows there's precious little of that.
Some say trading stamps are going out of style.
I'll collect them till I die.
At least it's something I do well.

Conversation on a Front Porch

Once my husband was out of the house, I thought that would be the end of it, but of course, it wasn't. Every Saturday morning, around six thirty, he'd show up out front and beg me to take him back. "After all," he'd say, "you said in sickness and in health. This is sickness. Take me back." But by then I had finally figured out that if eighteen years of my loving him hadn't fixed him, he wasn't going to get well.

People ask me why I moved from Phoenix to Seattle. I tell them, I was a refugee from a bad marriage and a worse divorce. The real reason I had to leave town was that I was weak and susceptible and every bit as addicted to my husband as he was to booze. Even waiting to meet him at a restaurant to discuss the terms of our divorce, I felt my heart rise in my throat at simply seeing the man walking toward me on the sidewalk. I was outraged that my body could betray me in such a fashion. He was bad for me. He had drained me of all joy and laughter, although I didn't know how thoroughly for a very long time.

Six years later, and a year into my marriage to my second

husband—the nice one—we visited Phoenix. I took my new husband by the insurance agency office where I had once worked to introduce him to the people who had been my fellow employees there. None of the people in the office recognized me because, in all the years we had worked together, they had never seen me smile and had never heard me laugh.

CONVERSATION ON A FRONT PORCH

He rings the doorbell. More distant
Than a stranger, he stands on the porch
Of the house that used to be our home,
Begging me to come and talk,
Just talk, he tells me, nothing more.

Civility is difficult to put away,
Especially after years of sharing lives.
And so I go. It's easier to go and listen
Than it is to say no. Saying no requires honesty,
A commodity that seems to be in very short supply.

I listen as he reviews mistakes, hoping to find
The key that will put things right again,
But time for that has long since passed, and now
Our only hope is to exit with perhaps
A modicum of grace.

At last I find a plausible excuse to go inside,
Placing welcome distance between his rosary of blame
And me. I will not go again to hear him tell his beads,
To say a mournful requiem over something
That has passed beyond all powers of resurrection.

Why?

I probably should have named this poem "Collateral Damage" instead of "Why?"

The kids were little when their father moved out of the house. My daughter was in first grade, my son in kindergarten. Since I was the one who had instigated the divorce, I was the one left to answer the children's questions, and I did that as best I could. I sat them down and read a book aloud to them, *The Boys and Girls Book About Divorce*.

More than thirty years later, the results are mixed. My daughter, seventeen months older than my son, remembers enough of what went on back then that she has been nothing but supportive, both of me and of my second husband. My son, on the other hand, still holds me responsible for what happened. And maybe I am.

I can see now that it was wrong of me to set out to save someone who wasn't interested in being saved. Marriage is not an urban renewal project. No one gave me the right to assume the mantle of Rescuer in Chief. But I did, and, in so doing, I reaped a whirlwind of unhappiness for any number of people—for myself and my husband, yes, but most of all, for my children.

Even after all this time, I still can't give them an answer any better than the one I gave them back then: because.

WHY?

I knew the time would come to give an answer,
To explain to childish hearts the reasons why.
No matter what I say I'll beg the question.
Part will be the truth and part a lie.

I hear myself say, "I no longer love him,"
Words too weak to justify the pain. I say,
"You know we both will always love you,"
But I know their lives will never be the same.

"Because," I say, and that's my final answer.
No further explanation will suffice.
Their eyes fill up with tears, my hands are shaking,
My heart's a heavy block of solid ice.

Insomnia

No matter the cause of that final separation—whether it be death or divorce—there's nothing worse in the aftermath of losing a spouse than trying to go to sleep. For years I had gone to bed cursing *Starsky & Hutch* and *Police Woman*. The only way my husband could sleep was with guns blazing and sirens wailing from the television set across the room. After he moved out, I tried to sleep with the TV switched off, but that didn't work. I tried sleeping with it on. No dice there, either.

In those restless, endless hours between lying down and going to sleep, we are tortured by the racket of a thousand if-onlys careening around in our heads—all the woulda, coulda, shoulda, mightas that wait to pounce in the middle of the night and send us staggering, sleepless, into another torturous day.

During the months before and after my divorce, the only place I could sleep was in church. I will be forever grateful to the late Reverend "Mac" McKinley of Encanto Congregational Church in Phoenix for his kindness and understanding when I nodded off during countless sermons that were probably wonderful. I seldom heard more than a few words before I was a goner. I know he noticed what was happening because one Sunday his sermon was entitled "On Sleeping in Church." I don't know what he said in that one, either, because I slept through it from beginning to end.

When the service was over, I tried to apologize. He shook my hand, smiled at me, and said, "Don't worry. You're coming to church and getting exactly what you need."

INSOMNIA

I prowl the house in search of errant sleep
Whose balm eludes me like some wily beast
Which easily avoids the hunter's snare.

The bed's to be untouched at any cost.
Too much of him is there, too much of me.
The cool sheets sting me with a burning grief.

I try a couch, the floor, and finally the chair,
But nowhere can I put my mind at rest,
Or lose myself in soothing, sweet repose.

For far too long I slept with my hip next to his,
His arm thrown randomly across my drowsing breast.
Will I ever learn to sleep again alone?

It's much too soon to tell.

Undying Love

I cannot quite recapture the depth of my misery in those first few months during and after my divorce. It must be the same kind of defense mechanism that makes it possible for women to forget the pain of childbirth and have more than one baby. I was alive, but just barely. I was divorced, but I was a long way from being over my husband. There are times even now when I'm not sure I'm over him yet. Although I've been happily married to my second husband for nearly twenty-eight years, my first one still intrudes in my dreams on occasion and leaves me shaken by the things he says and does.

I know what the King of Siam from *The King and I* would say: Is a puzzlement.

UNDYING LOVE

I cling to that past love with all the ferocity
Of a half-crazed mother
Who clutches her dead baby to her breast,
Refusing to give it up to other hands,
Hands that will carefully prepare the body
For its final bed.

The love is past but I cannot relinquish
Its claim upon my heart. I carry
The corpse with me where I go
And pray for the courage
To one day lay it down
And walk away.

After the Fire

By the time I divorced my husband, he had been hospitalized nine times for chronic alcoholism in the preceding seven years. The last time was at a rehab place in Wickenburg, Arizona. That I attended Family Week halfway through his six-week stay there testifies to the fact that, even though the divorce was in progress, I still thought I could "save" him. That didn't happen. He was drinking again within five days of being released. What did happen at the Wickenburg treatment center was nonetheless a miracle—for me.

All the other times my husband had been in treatment, I had gone along with the program and with whatever joint sessions were required, always in hopes of making him better. His counselors from Wickenburg kept calling and inviting me to Family Week. I told them that I was getting a divorce and that I didn't want to be his family anymore. I also had a job to do and children to care for and support. When I finally agreed to go, I told them I'd stay for only two of the seven days.

The first evening the counselor ended the family-member session by talking about Easter. He said that without Good Friday there would be no Easter Sunday. Without the crucifixion, there could be no resurrection. He advised us to go to our individual hotel rooms. We were told to spend the night alone with television sets and radios turned off. He said that if our loved ones were sick enough to be in treatment, then our lives had been in pain for a long time. We should simply lie on our beds, listen to our bodies, and try to figure out where we hurt.

I was skeptical at best, but since I had agreed to stay for the two days, I figured I might just as well try following the counselor's directions. So I went to my room, lay on the bed, and concentrated on my body. After a while, I realized that my jaw ached—no doubt from grinding my teeth—and my breastbone felt bruised and tender to the touch. Feeling my own physical pain resulted in an astounding revelation. Obviously this counselor, who had never met me before, knew things about me and my body that I hadn't known myself. And if he knew that much, there was probably a lot more that I needed to learn from him. I ended up calling home, canceling my appointments, and staying for the remainder of Family Week—all seven days.

That marked the beginning of my own recovery. It was during that week in Wickenburg when I first realized I was living "After the Fire."

AFTER THE FIRE

I have touched the fire.
It burned me, but I knew I lived.
It seared me, but it made me whole.

He called me.
I went gladly though I saw the rocks,
Fell laughing through the singeing air.

I have known the fire.
I'll live with nothing rather than with less.
The flame is out. There's nothing left but ash.

Unilateral Disarmament

One year after Family Week in Wickenburg, I was living in Seattle and trying to put my life back together. My daughter was in Girl Scouts. My son was once again playing T-ball. When his birthday came around that year, there was no present from his father, who was now living in New Mexico and working construction. I was utterly outraged. How could he forget such a thing? The next time we talked on the phone I lit into him about it, and several days later a tardy birthday present arrived.

With delight, my son opened the box and pulled out what I thought was a baseball bat. That evening he proudly took it to T-ball practice. Halfway through practice, one of the male coaches took me aside and asked why my son had brought a softball bat to baseball practice. I was stunned! Floored! Livid! I'm a liberal arts major who wore glasses and never played a sport in my life. My son's father was, in high school, a talented all-around athlete. I may not have known the difference, but he sure as hell did!

I went home from practice bristling with anger. Did he do it on purpose? Was it an accident? Did he do it to trick me? Those are questions that will never have satisfactory answers, and it drove me wild that even from more than seventeen hundred miles away, he could still push my buttons and send me into an emotional tailspin. The next time he called it was once again a telephone version of World War III. After that phone call, with atomic fallout still floating in the air, I wrote "Unilateral Disarmament."

UNILATERAL DISARMAMENT

Children are the weapons in this war,
And neither side is blameless of their use.
Armed with offhand remarks we send them forth
Oblivious to the damage that we do.

Who will sound retreat from battle lines
Or hammer out an end to bitter frays?
Continued fighting seems a coward's ploy,
But quitting will require all my strength.

Negotiated peace eludes me still,
Slipping from my grasp at every turn.
For my children's sake hostilities must end.
I leave my trench and turn to face the sun.

Death Sentence

At six thirty on Thanksgiving morning 1982, my former husband called to wish the kids a happy Thanksgiving. They were down the hall, asleep, as were my parents, who were visiting from Arizona. I told him it was too early to wake them up and asked him to call back later in the day. The remainder of the morning and all afternoon passed with no phone call. Finally, when we were in the middle of Thanksgiving dinner, he called back and railed at me for refusing to let him talk to his children earlier. While they were on the phone with him, I cleared the table, sweeping plates and silverware away and slamming them into the dishwasher before my guests had finished chewing their last bites. When I went to bed that night, I was still angry, and not just at him. I was furious at myself for continuing to allow myself to be suckered into the same old games.

Two days later my mother-in-law called to tell me that my former husband was in the hospital. She had come to visit him over Thanksgiving. In anticipation of her visit, he had tried to sober up. After months of steady drinking, he had gone off alcohol cold turkey and without being under a doctor's care. In the process, he had disrupted his metabolism. He had been found lying unconscious in the street in Tempe on Thanksgiving night and was taken to Scottsdale Memorial Hospital. At first doctors thought he had been struck by a car. Later examination revealed that he had gone into DTs. He was hospitalized with no liver or kidney function.

DEATH SENTENCE

He's dying.
Words come through the wire and hammer home
Despite the doctor's cloying, unctuous tone.

He's dying.
I thought my tears exhausted years ago,
And yet it hurts, oh God, how much it hurts!

He's dying.
This is what I wanted when I thought a widow's garb
Would suit me better than a court's decree.

He's dying.
Should I go to him or stay away?
What right have I to be there now?

He's dying.
I'll go.

Vigil

My former husband was hospitalized for over a month with his mother at his side. She called me daily with updates. I agonized about what to do. Should I send the children to see him or should I take them? And what about going myself? When I finally, tearfully, asked an old friend what I should do, she said, "Have you asked the children what they want?"

So I took the children out to dinner separately. I told each of them what I had been told—that their father was dying—and asked whether they wanted to go see him before it was too late. Individually they both decided against going. Finally, the day after Christmas and at my mother-in-law's urging, I went myself.

Walking into that hospital room, I was shocked to see my former husband's condition, and I was grateful the children had decided against coming. He was mostly unconscious by then and had wasted away to almost nothing. Out in the hall, I overheard a pair of doctors talking about him. Despite the fact that the man had been a patient in their hospital for over a month, the doctors and nurses were still mispronouncing his last name. I'm sure my mother-in-law had tried to correct this situation, but she was too worn down to fight anymore. I wasn't. I went out into the hall and lit into them about it. From then on, the hospital staff gave me a wide berth.

New Year's Eve came. Mary Grandma—as the children called their grandmother—had been at the hospital day in and day out for weeks. I insisted on taking her to a restaurant for dinner. When we came back to the room at about eight o'clock, a nurse told us that his blood pressure was falling.

VIGIL

We keep a vigil by his midnight bed,
His mother and his former wife,
Grieving for the man we loved and lost.
It's harder for his mother than for me.
I've already known the sting of loss.
She's only now begun to see she cannot win.

He's quiet now. A nurse comes in to loosen his restraints,
Not looking at the women waiting there.
She knows. She doesn't want to say.
The hours creep by. All stories are expended,
Yet we need some sound to hold the night at bay.
"Please sing," his mother asks me, and I do.

It is a serenade of love,
Of songs we knew and treasured through the years,
From bawdy barroom ditties to sweet hymns.
The hours flow by. We hold his hands.
I sing a line and wait to see if he will breathe again.
He doesn't. It's over. Amen.

Death After Divorce

When I agreed to go to Phoenix, I thought I was going to help my mother-in-law. Before his hospitalization, my former husband had been reduced to being little more than a bum on the street. I was the one who still had the Christmas card list and knew the names, addresses, and telephone numbers of the people who needed to be notified or asked to serve as pallbearers. What I didn't recognize—something I believe Mary Grandma did—was that my being there was important for me, too. Her son and I were divorced, but she understood that I needed to come and say good-bye, not so much because it would help him, but because it would help me.

I will always be grateful to her for that. It was an important gift, one that gave me the strength to pick up the pieces of my own life and go on.

DEATH AFTER DIVORCE

I come to widow's weeds unwed,
The tie that binds unraveled but still bound.
I sang a song to speed him on his way
And hoped he gained some comfort in the sound.

My love renewed in those brief final hours,
All rancor gone, all bitterness and grief,
And as I touched his cheek or soothed his brow,
We wrote the final chapter of our breach.

And as his painful struggle neared its end,
When ragged breath gave way to endless sleep,
We welcomed death together, he and I,
For granting us the blessing of release.

Missing Condolence

I met my first husband the evening before my eighteenth birthday. We were introduced by a mutual acquaintance from Bisbee who gave me a ride home from Tucson for the weekend. The two guys were on their way to go deer hunting, and the man who would be my husband lost a wager on me the first time he ever laid eyes on me. He had bet his friend a pitcher of beer that I wouldn't be ready to go, but I was. I was waiting in the vestibule of my dorm—packed, signed out, and ready to leave. Over the years we stayed friends with the guy who introduced us and, once he married, with his wife as well. When our son was born, his middle name was Mikki, in honor of our friend.

After my first husband's death, I received many expressions of condolence, but there was none from the man who had introduced us. I learned years later that he blamed me for my husband's death and claimed that his friend wouldn't have died had I not taken his beloved children away from him. It was easy for the friend to blame me. After all, he hadn't been at that baseball field watching my children's father crawling toward the car on his hands and knees.

MISSING CONDOLENCE

Pretty cards and thoughtful letters come
Bringing sympathy and comfort from our friends,
Both his and mine.

One is missing.
Daily I scan the envelopes for some sign
That his best friend forgives me,
That he accepts my present grief as real.

It does not come—no sign, no call, no word.
The loss of friendship pains me still,
An ache persisting in an amputated limb.

Mother's Day, 1983

I loved my mother-in-law. The only thing Mary Grandma and I had in common was her son, but even after the divorce we stayed in touch. I made sure she saw the children and talked to them on the telephone. After her son's death, that relationship continued. The following spring she came to Seattle to visit. The children and I took her to Butchart Gardens in Vancouver, British Columbia, but the light had gone out of her life, and she never regained the joy of living.

On June 12, 2000, my mother's middle son, my younger brother Jim, suffered a massive heart attack and died while swimming off Hermosa Beach in California. As I worked on these notes first in 2003, I realized that the words I wrote for Mary Grandma in 1983 now applied to my own mother as well. Evelyn Busk raised seven children. There are six of us left, but like that single envelope in "Missing Condolence," with first her beloved son and later her husband gone, much of the light went out of my mother's last years as well.

MOTHER'S DAY, 1983

To be mother when a child is gone
Beyond reach of touch or drop of tear,
Is grief that only a mother can know
And pain that only a mother can bear.

You gave him life and watched him play.
You brought him up as best you knew.
Yet, headstrong, he would choose his way,
And there was nothing you could do,

But love him, and we know you did—
Loved him with love unstinting, free.
You loved him enough to let him go.
You loved him enough to let him be.

And though this special day, I know,
Will not pass by without a tear,
We wanted to tell you we love you so,
And through that love, he can still be here.

Building a Legend

I remember my husband telling me that it didn't matter if he drank; he was only hurting himself. That's nonsense, of course. He was killing himself, but he was also hurting all the rest of us—the people who loved him, his children and his wife. He moved out of the house in 1980, we were divorced in 1981, and he died in December 1982. Time has passed, but much of what I wrote in "Building a Legend" in 1983 still holds true today. One of my children has moved beyond what happened back then. One is still trapped by his unwavering belief in the legend. My son harbors a legacy of blame that holds me responsible for everything that happened and for everything that went wrong. I believe both his parents were at fault.

I like to think that someday we'll be over this hurt, but at this point, I don't hold out much hope.

BUILDING A LEGEND

It's easy now for him to be a hero.
He's moved beyond the reach of new mistakes.
In legend he is twice as big as life-size,
And the things he did were honorable and great.

It's easy too to make him out a villain,
There's no one here to speak in his defense.
If I give each act a black and hidden motive,
Who would care or know the difference?

Then let me find the middle ground between them,
These two opposing views of one who's gone.
And when I tell the children of their father,
Let me lighten truth with just a hint of sun.

Kindred Spirit

If you're married when a spouse dies, there are certain rules that govern your behavior. The grieving widow or widower knows generally what is expected, and other people have some idea of what they should say or do and how they, too, should behave. If you're divorced and a former spouse dies, all those rules go out the window.

Months after my husband's death, I was on the opposite side of this thorny issue when a good friend of mine died. She had been an invalid for years. She and her husband had long been estranged, but due to health insurance and financial considerations, divorce simply wasn't possible for either of them.

I had listened sympathetically to my friend's side of the story as her marriage disintegrated. At the time of her death, I was still angry with her husband and ready to blame him for abandoning her emotionally if not financially. Still, when she died, I couldn't help remembering how I had felt the previous year, when I was the one looking for that missing sympathy card—the one that never came. Bearing that in mind, I straightened up and sent my friend's estranged husband a card. Then I sat down and wrote "Kindred Spirit"—for me.

KINDRED SPIRIT

I leaped to name another's grief as false,
To claim his tears as crocodile or worse.
I laid my friend's flown spirit at his door
And called for him to know his just deserts.

Yet as the words of judgment crossed my mind,
I recalled when that same charge was hurled at me,
When after years of pain and separation,
Death came home, with love, to set us free.

So instead of blame, I offer consolation.
Instead of hurt, I give him hope and love.
The giver with the gift is overtaken
While blessings flow to me as from above.

Fog

By September 1983, I was beginning to feel better. I was living in Seattle and still selling life insurance but also starting to write mysteries. The first novel I wrote, in 1982, never sold to anyone. The second one was accepted by the first agent and sold to the second editor who saw it. I wrote every morning from four to seven, at which time I would awaken the children and send them off to school. Then I would get myself ready to go to work. I was involved in several civic organizations in Seattle, including the Denny Regrade Business Association, where I served on the committee that planted street trees in the Regrade area in the early 1980s.

One of those civic organizations met in the early morning for breakfast. Going to a meeting one fall day, I walked downhill in fog so thick that I could barely see half a block in front of me. Being from the Arizona desert, I was totally unfamiliar with this phenomenon. Somehow I had always imagined that fog and rain went together. That particular morning, however, I came out of the meeting less than an hour later and was astonished to discover that the fog had burned away, leaving a clear blue sky overhead.

FOG

I walk in fog.
Its velvet touch caresses me
And hides the hurt.
Beyond the fog, the sun
Shines clear and bright.
I must keep moving,
I have earned the light.

Walking Wounded

In early 1985 an old friend came to Seattle to visit. His marriage had recently dissolved. We had coffee and talked. There was never any hint of romance between us—it was more a matter of talking together and comparing notes. Somehow, though, by the end of that conversation, I knew I was moving in the right direction—knew I was getting better.

WALKING WOUNDED

He is a long-lost friend who comes to town.
We meet to talk about old times.
The years between this meeting and the last
Have cost us both the people that we loved.

It takes a while to melt the ice, to take away
The distance passing years can interpose.
Once the ice floe breaks, we find that we are
Veterans of the same far-reaching war.

Our scars aren't visible to naked eyes,
But underneath a bland façade
We both are hiding wounds that won't be healed
By anything but time's slow steps.

When our talk is over, we take in hand
Our bandaged hearts and hopes and go
Our separate ways. Maybe when we meet again
The present tense will offer more allure,
And we will leave the past where it belongs.

He goes, but subtle changes have occurred within,
A hint that springtime's thaw is under way
And flowers are pushing through the glacier's edge.

Maiden Names

Growing up in Bisbee, Arizona, I had three special childhood friends. Donna Angeleri was the first. She lived at the top of Yuma Trail, and we spent summer afternoons clambering barefoot through the desert that lined the far side of our street. We coasted down the hilly roadway with a maximum load of four kids packed into our Radio Flyer wagon. When I was in the third grade the Angeleris moved to California, and I never heard from Donna again.

In fourth grade I met Pat McAdams. We were pals all through school and coeditors of our high school newspaper, *The Copper Chronicle*. School, marriage, kids, and divorce took their toll on our friendship over the years, but now, through the magic of the Internet, Pat and I are back in communication almost every day.

Diana Conway arrived in Bisbee the summer I entered sixth grade. Her family moved into the newly remodeled house that had once belonged to the Angeleris. They lived there for a grand total of three months. The Conways were sophisticated oddballs in small-town Arizona. The kids called their parents Joe and Sally. They all rode bikes at a time when no other grown-ups in Bisbee would have been caught dead riding a bicycle. They all loved books, and Diana played the piano wonderfully. Without any noticeable nagging from her parents, she practiced at least four hours every day.

At the end of that summer the Conways, too, moved to California. I visited them once, the summer after eighth grade, catching a train from Tucson and traveling out to see them. Diana and I corresponded for years after that, but shortly after we graduated from college, we lost track of each other. When my first hardback, *Hour of the Hunter,* was published, in 1991, I dedicated it to "Diana Conway, wherever she is," in hopes of finding my long-lost friend. For years nothing happened. Then in 2001, a fan of mine asked about the dedication. It turned out that one of her good friends in Alaska was my missing friend. Since then, Diana and I have picked up the threads of our childhood friendship. And it turns out, my poem was right; our paths have been in parallel. Diana, too, is a writer.

MAIDEN NAMES

To Diana Conway from Judy Busk

We were young girls together,
Eleven or twelve at most,
Yet our conversations soared to galaxies afar.

We carried books by wagonload,
Dug for fossils, climbed a rock or two
And swore that they were mountains.

We lost each other later in a maze
Of married names that easily removed all trace
Of those two friends together.

I think of you, Diana, and I know
Our paths must be in parallel.
I only hope someday they'll cross again.

Changing Times

My youngest brother, Gary, was an impressionable high school student when I was at my fiercest, most fire-breathing feminist stage. He made a key ring for me in welding shop and gave it to me forty years ago, when I was teaching on the reservation. I still have it. I am working on my laptop in the living room. The key ring is in the kitchen, resting in the top drawer with my other keys and a haphazard collection of coupons and Ziploc bags.

I still treasure the key ring, but when I look at it now, I no longer see what is missing.

CHANGING TIMES

My brother made the key ring years ago,
The female symbol with a welded fist
Clenched in the defiant gesture of that time.

The fist broke later, I don't know when,
And for years it stayed that way,
Half broken like some long-forgotten grudge.

Eventually it disappeared—not the ring, the fist,
And when I noticed it was gone,
I laughed, because I, too, had changed.

Interim

I wrote this poem in June 1984, not knowing that in June 1985 my life would take a sudden turn for the better when I would meet the man who would become my second husband six months to the day from the day we met. I think the long period of quiet, not only after my divorce but also after my former husband's death, put me in better emotional shape for what was to come.

For those who are unfamiliar with the Arizona desert, it is helpful to know that the heat of summer usually comes in early June. By July the desert is parched and the trees and plants seem dead or dying. Then the rains come, and life returns. Perhaps people back east or in the Midwest—people who live with snow and real winter weather—have the same kind of reaction to spring, but for desert rats, life begins anew when thunderclouds come racing up from the south, bringing with them life-sustaining rain.

INTERIM

The part of me that's woman has removed
To some far distant place
And there awaits a time when I can once more
Dare the risk and hurt of love.

It's quiet here and calm, the stillness of a stagnant pond
Before the summer rains bring surging life.
It's June. The storms will come in mid-July.
By then I will have waited long enough.

Daybreak

I have little patience with people who consider themselves experts in how long the grief process should last. People who haven't lived through that soul-numbing pain, and even some who have, often act as though there is a certain time by which a grief-stricken person should simply shape up and quit "wallowing" in it. They don't have the time or patience to listen when someone needs to talk and ruminate about what happened. Interestingly enough, these are often the very same people who feel free to wag fingers and point out that someone certainly "got over it in a hurry." They have no concept that many survivors, having battled some slow killer like cancer or Alzheimer's, have done their grieving well in advance—long before death finally made its final curtain-lowering entrance.

However long it takes, or however short, there comes a day when the survivor opens his or her eyes and realizes that it is morning at last. The sun has come up, and life really does go on. When that happens—when the gray gloom finally brightens a little and one catches that first hint of blue sky—it seems like an incredible miracle, and it is—the same kind of miracle that makes spring follow winter and sunrise follow night.

DAYBREAK

Love has come full circle, and I know
That I am free to live again at last,
Without my every waking breath and moment
Haunted by some image from the past.

With my heart closed and clutching our transgressions,
Old hates and hurts could never fall away.
But now the door is slowly creaking open.
At peace, in joy, I rise to greet the day.

Benediction

This final poem is actually out of sequence, but benedictions are traditionally last, and this one is last for that reason. It was written in the early 1980s, when the promise it expresses seemed an impossible dream. Considering what was going on in my life at that time, it's not surprising that I drew on my past to write it.

The year I was a sophomore at the University of Arizona, I came down with a urinary tract infection that was severe enough to send me to the infirmary. Early the next morning, shortly after I awakened, my then boyfriend appeared, carrying in his hand a single rose that he had purloined from someone's garden on his way to see me. It was a dusty pink color with a few sparkling dewdrops still lingering on the petals. That rose is something I've never forgotten. In fact if I close my eyes right now I can see the tender petals and the dewdrops still gleaming like diamonds in the early morning sunlight.

BENEDICTION

I gave the Lord my greatest grief,
My burden, and my care.
He turned it over like a leaf,
And soon there blossomed there,
A flower of faith, a bloom of grace,
With petals soft and fair.
The dewdrop sparkling in the sun
Was once, I'm sure, a tear.

My life was storm-tossed and confused,
I couldn't find my way.
I asked the Lord to see me through
And guide me day by day.
He took my hand and calmed the sea,
Waves died at His command.
Then o'er the calm He carried me
Until we reached dry land.

And as the storm clouds rolled away,
Their edges silver lined,
I watched a rainbow bridge the sky
And knew God's grand design.
He changes weakness into strength,
Makes courage from despair.
Our stumbling feet turn into wings,
When we come to Him in prayer.

Postscript

The life I live now often seems like a miracle. More than three decades after starting my long-delayed writing career, I still love writing. Almost twenty-eight years after marrying for the second time, my husband and I both cannot believe our good fortune in falling in love and marrying without wasting any precious time in the process. We have lived every day to the fullest, probably due in large measure to our mutual history. We came into this relationship with our hearts broken and with our dreams shattered. We both knew that life is not forever and that we have to make the most of whatever time we have.

We have homes in two places that we both love, Tucson and Seattle. In Seattle people who hear me being interviewed on the radio or television recognize me by my laughter—the same laughter that was totally absent from my earlier life in Phoenix. I went to Seattle in July 1981 as a single parent of two children. In 1985, after marrying again, I added a husband and three more children. Through the years we have been blessed with six grandchildren and a number of very spoiled dogs.

There are times when I feel a whole lot like a modern-day Cinderella, but the poems in this book, the ones I took with me to that widowed retreat back in 1985, were vitally important to this happy ending. If some of my readers are struggling with similarly tough issues, I hope they'll find hope and inspiration here.

I've come a very long way since 1980, when I wrote "The Collector" and thought that the best I could hope for in life was to collect trading stamps.

As I prepare this third edition of *After the Fire* for publication, it's early spring 2013. When my editor asked me to make some revisions, I was shocked to discover that the file containing the original version of this book was still on some long-ago PC rather than on my current MacBook Air. So, for the past two days, I've spent hours dictating both the poems and the accompanying essays, word by word, into my iPad. I'm hoping I've caught all those pesky auto-corrects, but I'm not sure. I have to say, Siri isn't much of a poet.

In the process I have been both surprised and gratified to learn that the poetry I wrote starting forty years ago still speaks to me, and I trust it will speak to others as well. The events portrayed in these poems may have happened in the distant past, but the benefits of those challenging experiences are present with me every day of my life. Living through tough times and learning the lessons they had to teach are what made me the person and the writer I am today.

I had a chemistry teacher who told me once, "All steps are necessary; no steps may be skipped." That's as true of life as it is of chemistry, and *After the Fire* is a book full of steps not skipped.